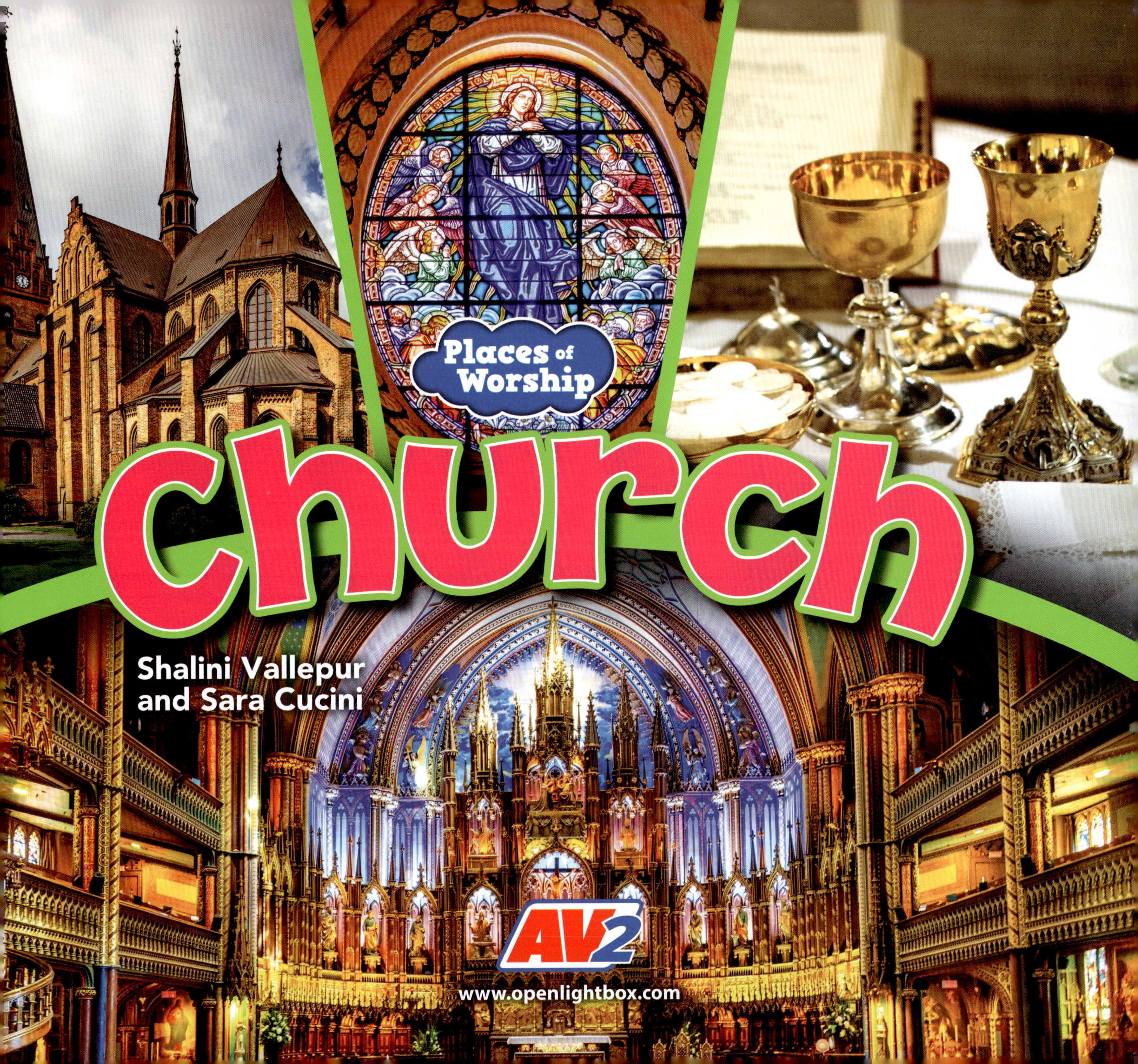

Places of Worship

Church

Shalini Vallepur
and Sara Cucini

AV2
www.openlightbox.com

AV2

Step 1
Go to **www.openlightbox.com**

Step 2
Enter this unique code
ZFEITBPVW

Step 3
Explore your interactive eBook!

AV2 is optimized for use on any device

Your interactive eBook comes with...

- **Audio** (Read) – Listen to the entire book read aloud
- **Videos** – Watch informative video clips
- **Weblinks** – Gain additional information for research
- **Try This!** – Complete activities and hands-on experiments
- **Key Words** – Study vocabulary, and complete a matching word activity
- **Quizzes** – Test your knowledge
- **Slideshows** – View images and captions
- **Share** – Share titles within your Learning Management System (LMS) or Library Circulation System
- **Citation** – Create bibliographical references following APA, CMOS, and MLA styles

This title is part of our AV2 digital subscription

1-Year K–5 Subscription
ISBN 978-1-7911-3320-7

Access hundreds of AV2 titles with our digital subscription.
Sign up for a FREE trial at **www.openlightbox.com/trial**

The digital components of this book are guaranteed to stay active for at least five years from the date of publication.

Places of Worship

Church

CONTENTS

Worship with Me

Have you ever been to a church? A church is a building of **worship** for followers of Christianity. Christians follow the teachings of Jesus Christ.

Christianity began about **2,000 years** ago.

In churches, ministers such as priests, pastors, rectors, or vicars lead prayers and **services**. They teach lessons from the Christian holy book, the **Bible**.

Welcome to the Church

There are different denominations, or kinds, of Christianity around the world. This means that some churches look very different from others.

Many churches have colorful stained glass windows. Some of the windows show stories from the Bible.

Some churches have bells. The **bells** ring to let worshipers know when services are happening.

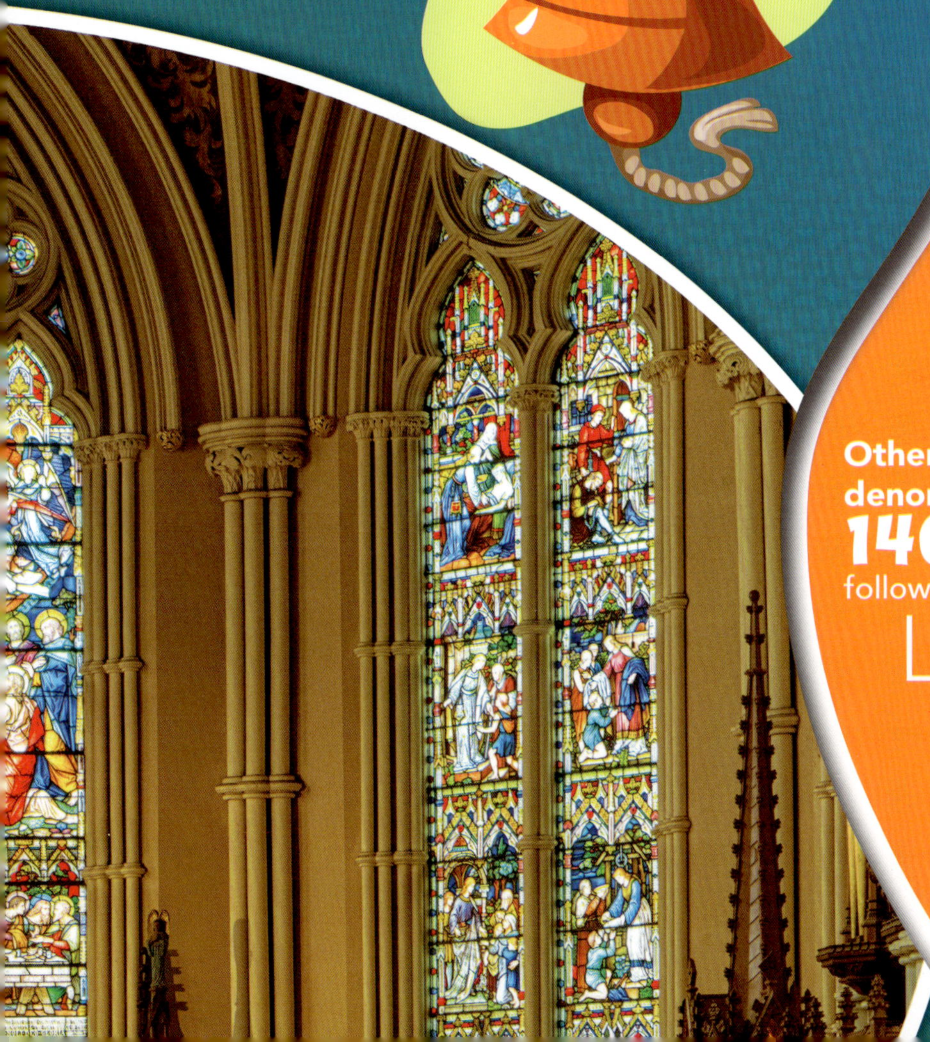

Christian Denominations

Inside the Church

Worshipers sit in the nave of a church. This is a large area that has many seats called pews.

When seated, worshipers face an area called the sanctuary.

There are many important items in the sanctuary.

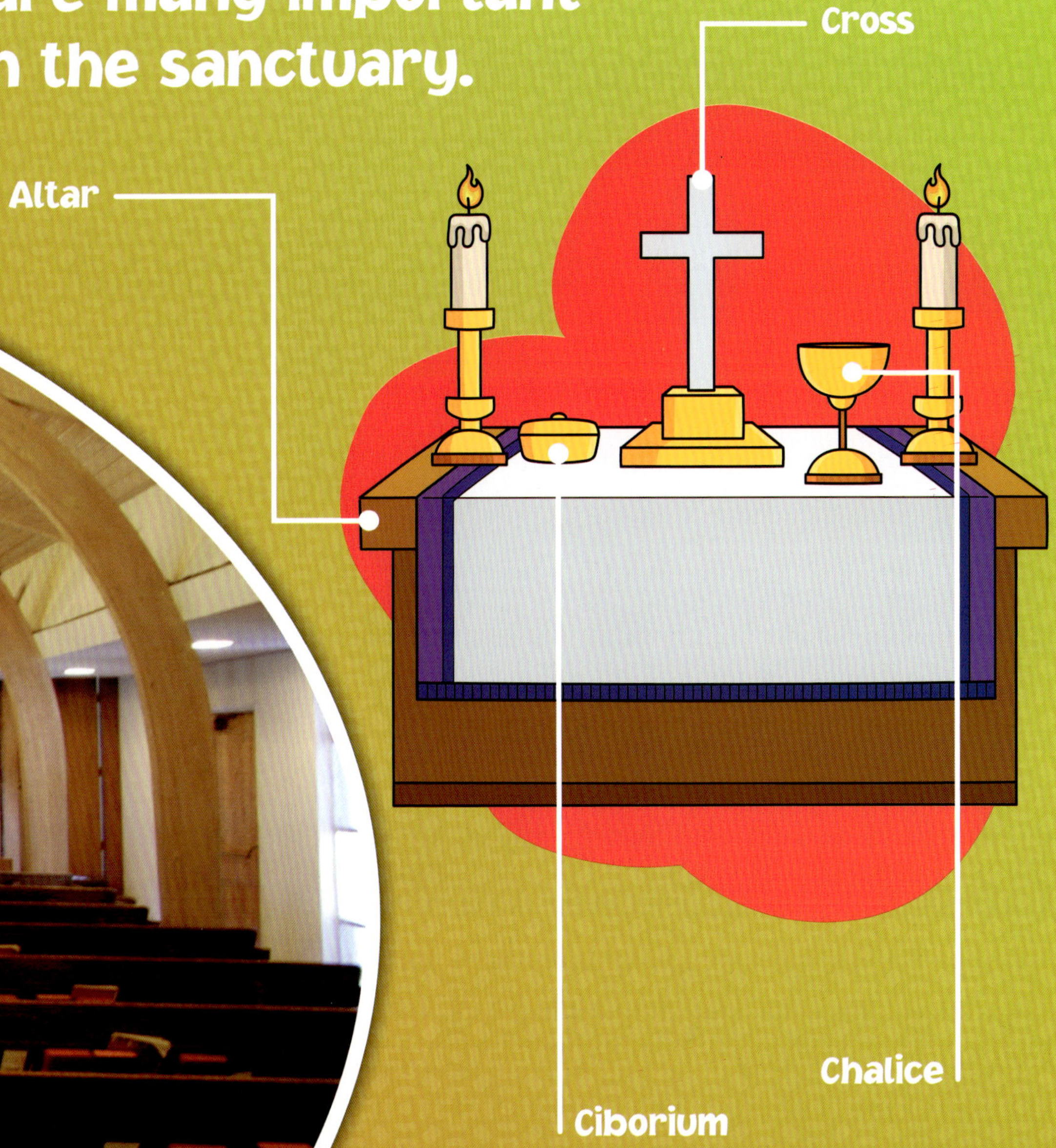

The Altar

The altar is a table. It is used during a service called **Holy Communion**. The altar reminds worshipers that Jesus Christ **gave** his life so that they may be saved.

During Holy Communion, worshipers walk up to the altar and are given **bread** and **wine**.

Holy Communion is also called the Eucharist, Mass, or the Lord's Supper.

Pulpits and Lecterns

The **pulpit** is usually in front of the sanctuary, facing the nave. It is a raised area that the priest uses when giving **sermons**.

The Bible is usually kept on a lectern. Ministers stand at the lectern and read the Bible to worshipers or lead prayers.

The Font

Fonts are usually found at the front of a church. **Holy water** is put into the font and used during a **baptism**.

Baptism is important to Christians. It is a sign of a person's faith in front of the Christian **community**.

Prayers and Hymns

Praying is a way for Christians to talk to God. Some Christians pray silently while others speak out loud.

Hymns are religious songs. They are often sung in churches as a form of worship.

The Lord's Prayer

"Our Father in Heaven, hallowed be your name, your kingdom come, your will be done, on Earth as it is in Heaven.

Give us today our daily bread. And forgive us our debts, as we also have forgiven our debtors.

And lead us not into temptation, but deliver us from the evil one."

(Matthew 6:9-13)

Sunday Service

Sunday is a day of worship. Many Christians go to church in the morning for **Sunday service**.

During the service, the minister may lead prayers, read from the Bible, and deliver a **sermon** from the pulpit. Hymns are usually sung.

Christmas

Christmas is a festival that remembers the birth of Jesus Christ. Midnight mass is a service that starts the night before Christmas.

Hymns are sung, and prayers are said during midnight mass. Some churches light many candles. Holy Communion happens, too.

Some churches recreate the Nativity using little figures.

Churches around the World

Saint Peter
Vatican City, Vatican
Catholic Church

Saint John the Divine
New York, United States
Episcopalian Church

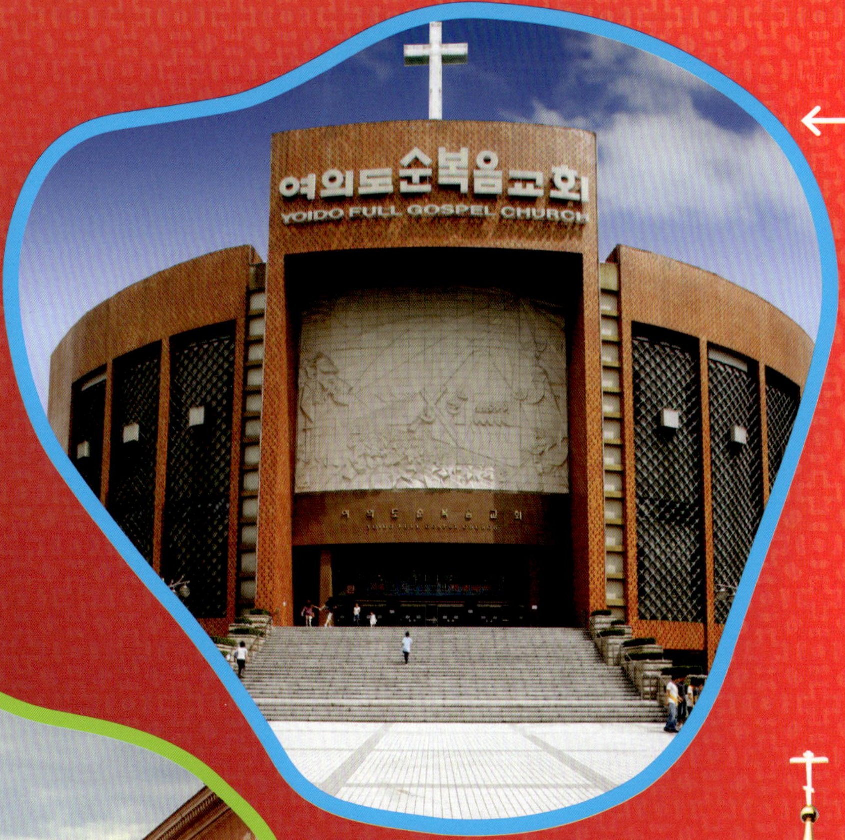

Yoido Full Gospel Church
Seoul, South Korea
Pentecostal Church

Saint Basil
Moscow, Russia
Eastern Orthodox Church

KEY WORDS

Research has shown that as much as 65 percent of all written material published in English is made up of 300 words. These 300 words cannot be taught using pictures or learned by sounding them out. They must be recognized by sight. This book contains 91 common sight words to help young readers improve their reading fluency and comprehension. This book also teaches young readers several important content words, such as proper nouns.

Page	Sight Words First Appearance
4	a, about, been, began, follow, for, have, is, me, of, the, to, with, years, you
5	and, as, book, from, in, or, such, they
6	are, around, different, kinds, look, many, means, others, show, some, that, there, this, very, world
7	know, let, when
8	an, face, has, large
9	important
10	be, his, it, life, may, so
11	also, up, walk
12	uses
13	at, on, read
14	found, into, put, water
16	often, out, songs, talk, way, while
17	but, come, Earth, Father, give, name, not, one, our, us, we, will, your
18	day, go
20	before, night, starts
21	light, little, said, too

Page	Content Words First Appearance
4	building, Christianity, Christians, church, followers, Jesus Christ, teachings, worship
5	Bible, lessons, ministers, pastors, prayers, priests, rectors, services, vicars
6	denominations, windows
7	Anglicanism, bells, Catholicism, Eastern Orthodoxy, Protestantism, worshipers
8	area, nave, pews, sanctuary, seats
9	altar, chalice, ciborium, cross, items
10	Holy Communion
11	bread, Eucharist, Lord's Supper, Mass, table, wine
12	lecterns, pulpits, sermons
14	baptism, font
15	community, faith, person, sign
16	God, hymns
17	debtors, debts, Heaven, kingdom, Matthew, temptation
18	morning, Sunday
20	birth, Christmas, festival
21	candles, figures, Nativity

Published by Lightbox Learning Inc.
276 5th Avenue, Suite 704 #917
New York, NY 10001
Website: www.openlightbox.com

Library of Congress Control Number: 2024935530

ISBN 978-1-5105-8181-4 (hardcover)
ISBN 979-8-8745-1509-6 (softcover)
ISBN 978-1-5105-8182-1 (static multi-user eBook)
ISBN 978-1-5105-8184-5 (interactive multi-user eBook)

Printed in Guangzhou, China
1 2 3 4 5 6 7 8 9 0 28 27 26 25 24

052024
100923

Project Coordinator: Sara Cucini
Designer: Jean Faye Rodriguez

Every reasonable effort has been made to trace ownership and to obtain permission to reprint copyright material. The publisher would be pleased to have any errors or omissions brought to its attention so that they may be corrected in subsequent printings.

The publisher acknowledges Getty Images and Shutterstock as the primary image suppliers for this title.

First published by BookLife in 2020.